D1742679

A BRONTOSAURUS CHORUS

A BRONTOSAURUS CHORUS

Edited by
Catherine Baker

Illustrated by Tony Ross

Methuen Children's Books

First published in Great Britain 1991
by Methuen Children's Books
Michelin House, 81 Fulham Road, London SW3 6RB
This compilation copyright © 1991 Catherine Baker
Illustrations copyright © 1991 Tony Ross

Printed in Great Britain
by St Edmundsbury Press, Bury St Edmunds, Suffolk.

British Library Cataloguing in Publication Data

A Brontosaurus chorus.
  I. Baker, Catherine II. Ross, Tony *1938–*
  821.91408

  ISBN 0–416–17632–1

Contents

Brontosaurus
Gail Kredenser

The giant Brontosaurus
Was a prehistoric chap
With four fat feet to stand on
And a very skimpy lap.
The scientists assure us
Of a most amazing thing —
A brontosaurus blossomed
When he had a chance to sing!

(The bigger brontosauruses,
Who liked to sing in choruses,
Would close their eyes
And harmonise
And sing most anything.)

They growled and they yowled,
They deedled and they dummed,
They warbled and they whistled,
They howled and they hummed.
They didn't eat, they didn't sleep;
They sang and sang all day.
Now all you'll find are footprints
Where they tapped the time away!

So Big
Max Fatchen

The dinosaur, an ancient beast,
I'm told, was very large.
His eyes were big as billiard balls,
His stomach, a garage.
He had a huge and humping back,
A neck as long as Friday.
I'm glad he lived so long ago
And didn't live in my day!

In China
Mark Burgess

My friend and I in China saw
A great big wobbly dinosaur.
We hadn't seen him there before,
That wobbly dinosaur.

We looked him up in our thesaurus;
He was a pronto-brontosaurus.
He did some wobbly dancing for us
Upon a parquet floor.

And then he came and bowed before us.
We clapped and shouted out *Encorus*.
He was the highlight of our *tourus*,
That wobbly dinosaur.

Tell all you know about . . .
Margaret Ryan

Triceratops was a dinosaur
With three horns upon his head.
He lived fifty million years ago
Give or take a day, it's said.
He roamed near swamps and marshes
He ate green leaves from trees.
That's all I know about him.
Can I go now, please?

I'd Never Dine on Dinosaurs
Jack Prelutsky

I'd never dine on dinosaurs,
they can't be good to eat,
for all they've got are lots of bones,
and not a bit of meat.

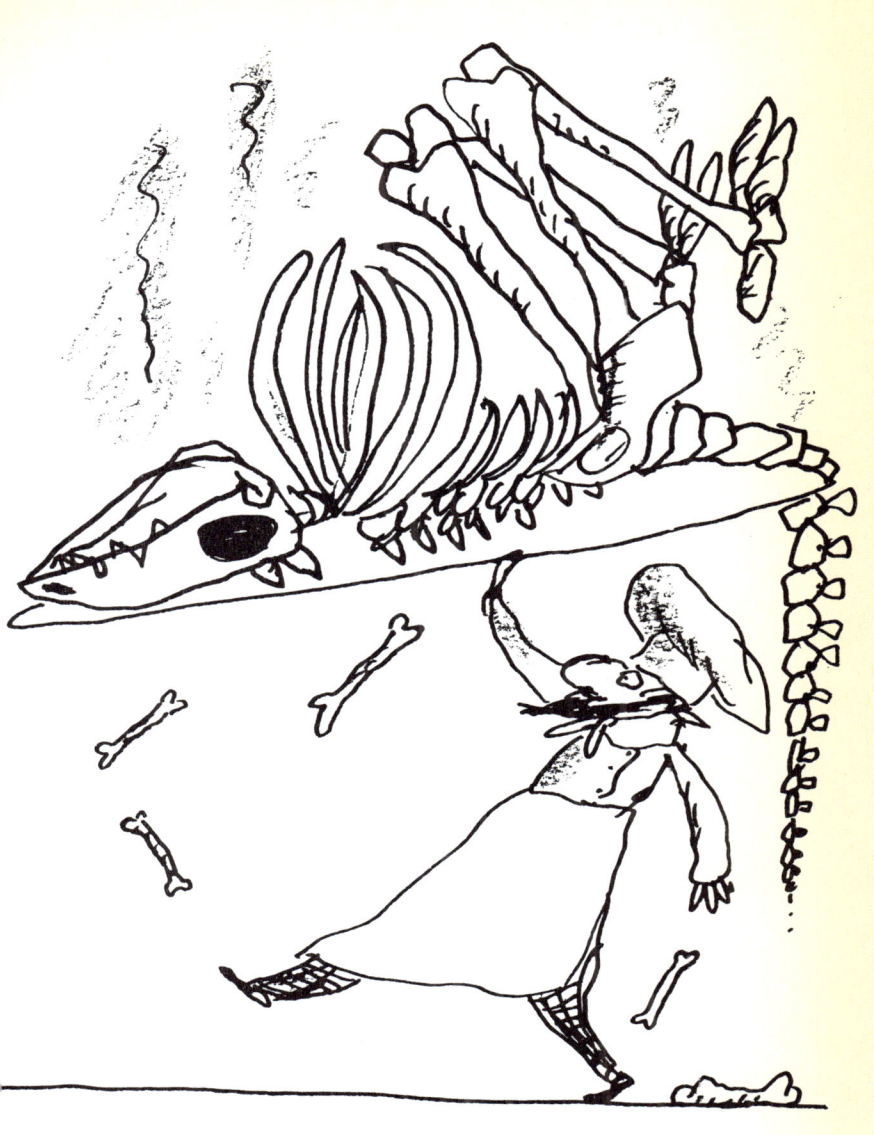

Tricky Archaeopteryx
Andrew Matthews

Most dinosaurs are awful bores
With gleaming fangs and pointed claws.
They stamp around and shake the ground
And make a dreadful roaring sound.
But I'm an archaeopteryx
And I can do some fancy tricks!

Most dinosaurs have massive jaws –
Especially tyrannosaurs!
But archaeopteryxes are
The prettiest dinosaurs by far,
With feathered wings and feathered tails
Instead of nasty lizard scales.

And if a stegosaur nearby
Regards me with a hungry eye,
I flap my wings and take a leap
And up into the air I sweep,
For I'm an archaeopteryx
And I can do some fancy tricks!

Lament
Derek Sampson

It isn't fun to be a brontosaurus.
There's nothing much to do but stand and stare.
After all it's hard to run
When your feet weigh half a ton
And you're dressed in armour-plated underwear.

We're so ugly other animals ignore us.
Our necks are like a giant teapot spout,
We have wrinkled yellow skins,
Bulging eyes and shovel chins
And what should be outside-in is inside-out.

The lives we have to lead completely bore us.
We never have an interesting time.
We just stand around and chomp
In a horrid smelling swamp
On disgusting lumps of weed and loads of slime.

If only there were someone who'd adore us,
Who'd stroke our necks and want to be our chum.
But there isn't, so that's that.
We're just stupid slow and fat.
Is it any wonder that we're always glum?

So if you ever meet a brontosaurus,
Be kind and pat his side and wipe his eye.
If you're cruel to him or frown
Then you're liable to drown.
Have you ever seen a brontosaurus cry?

A Big Brontosaurus
Barbara Ireson

A big Brontosaurus lay counting
As he breathed from the top of his head —
He started at one,
And when he was done,
'I'm two hundred years old!' he said.

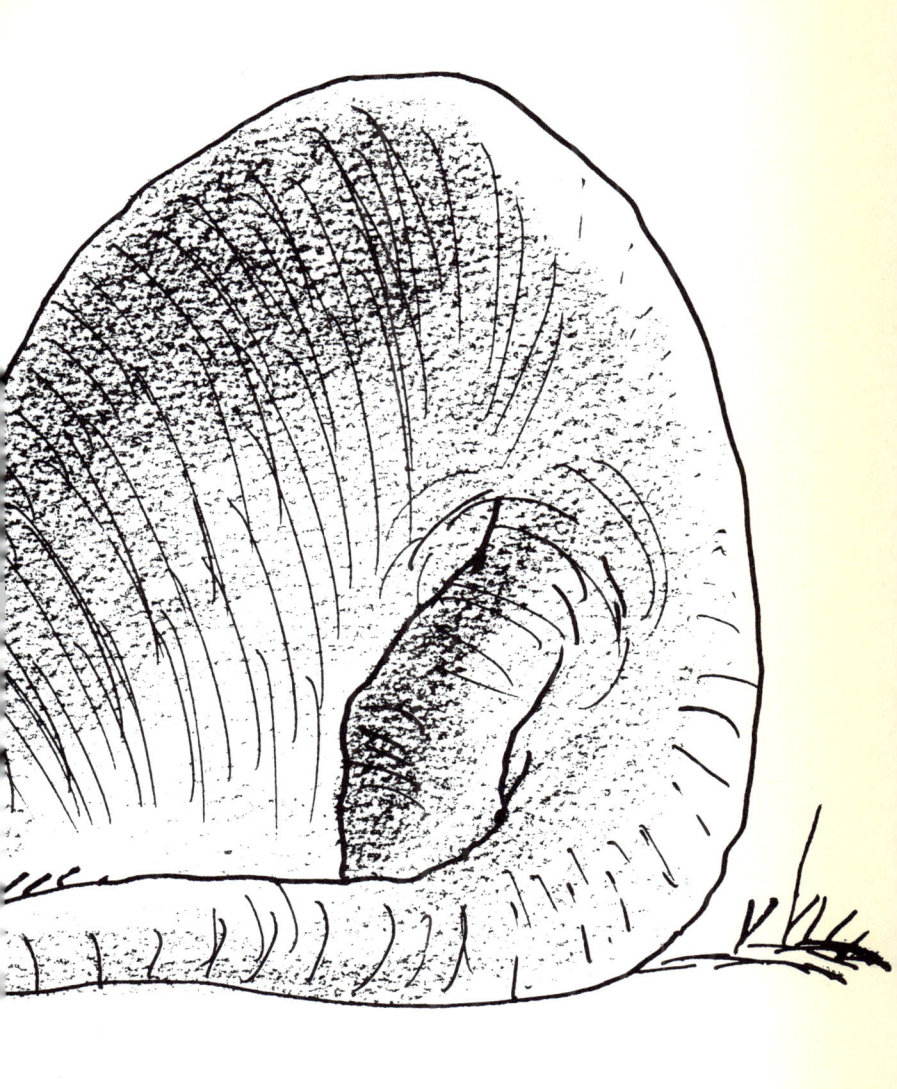

Lizard
Grace Nichols

A lean wizard –
watch me slither
up and down
the breadfruit tree
sometimes pausing a while
for a dither in the sunshine

The only thing
that puts a jitter up my spine
is when I think about
my great great great
great great great great
great great grandmother
Dinosaura Diplodocus

She would have the shock of her life
if she were to come back
and see me reduced to lizardsize!

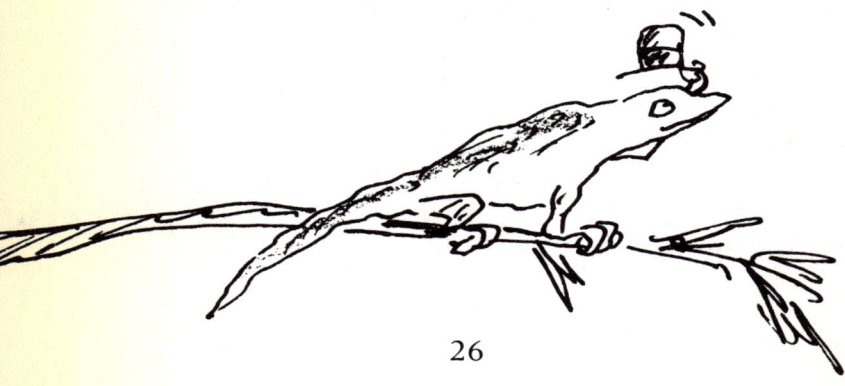

Pterodactyl
Roger McGough

Goodness gracious!
The pterodactyl
won't be back till
the next Cretaceous.

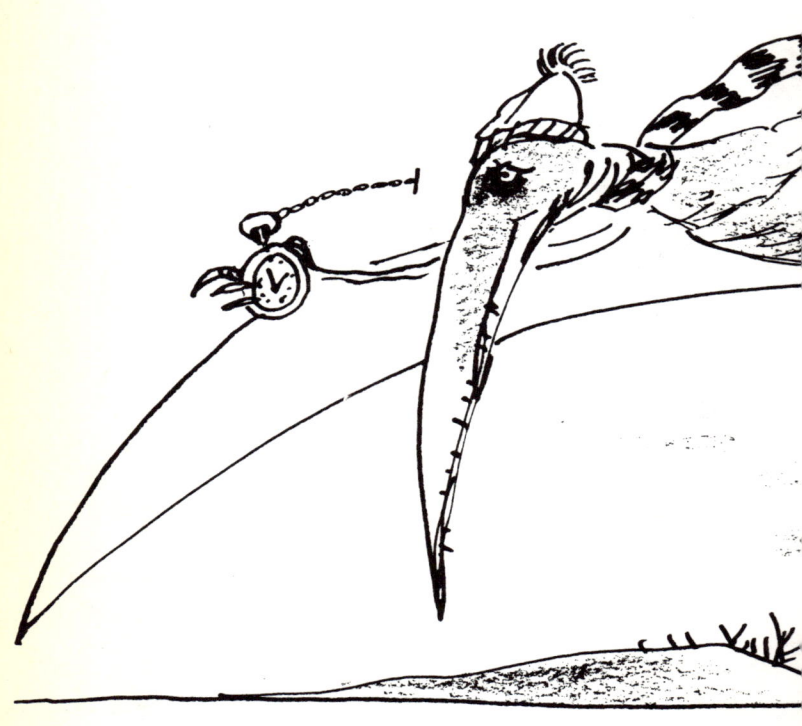

Destiny Dinosaur
W.J. Corbett

Destiny Dinosaur worshipped his dad
He wanted to be like him.
How he wished he could drink all alone a lake dry
Gaze fearlessly into an enemy's eye . . .
But Destiny's lungs and his legs were too small
And Daddy was ever so, ever so tall.
So to look a lot older, he stood on a boulder,
But only came up to his daddy's broad shoulder.

Destiny Dinosaur copied his dad
He tried to be just like him.
He followed him faithfully on to the plain
Where they stuck in the mud when it started to rain.
But Destiny's heart and his love were not small
For while sinking, he tried to look ever so tall,
With his toes on a boulder to look a lot older
But still only reaching his daddy's broad shoulder.

Destiny Dinosaur close to his dad
So ever so close to him,
For their bones are on permanent public display
And the children who goggle can sense his dismay
For Destiny's dreams on the plain took a blow
As he died with his Dad, as he started to grow . . .
There he stands on his boulder to look a lot older
A little less tall than his daddy's broad shoulder.

Where the Dinosaur Still Roams
Hiawyn Oram

Two hundred million years have passed
And still we hear the sound
Of Gentle Giants and Tyrant Kings
And Horned Heads thundering round
Two hundred million years have passed
And still we hear the roars
As Spiny Beasts like Armoured Tanks
Get torn by Terrible Claws
The dinosaur may be extinct
As all their bones will tell
The dinosaur may be extinct
And some say just as well
But there are still some dark forests
Lush with ginkgo trees and ferns
There are still rolling deserts
Where the sand's so hot it burns
There are still some conditions
Conjured up by fossil finds
Where the dinosaur's alive and roams
Forever – in our minds

My Heterodontosaurus
Leon Rosselson

Sam's a Diplodocus fan, he loves their snaky necks.
My brother pins up pictures of Tyrannosaurus Rex.
There are horny ones and frilly ones and ones with
knobbly scales
And ones I wouldn't like to meet with spikes upon
their tails.
But of all the curious creatures in that far-fetched
family
The Heterodontosaurus
The Heterodontosaurus
The Heterodontosaurus is the dinosaur for me.

My dinosaur's a dancer, she's nimble and she's neat
As she dances down to meet me on her dainty, birdy
feet,
As she dances round to greet me with her cheeky,
beaky grin,
And she gurgles when I tickle where she hasn't got a
chin
And I feed her flower sandwiches and leaves fresh
from the tree
Cos my Heterodontosaurus
My Heterodontosaurus
My Heterodontosaurus is the dinosaur for me.

And sometimes when she's very bored she likes a
    special treat
So she looks around the kitchen for anything that's
    sweet.
Then she'll swallow tubs of ice-cream and cakes that
    Mum's just made
And waterfalls of strawberries and lakes of lemonade.
Last week she ate my brother's birthday smarties for
    her tea
Yes, my Heterodontosaurus
My Heterodontosaurus
My Heterodontosaurus is the dinosaur for me.

It isn't that she's greedy and I tell my mum and dad
That she's only being mischievous, she isn't really bad.
But Dad gets quite excited and his face goes cherry
    red,
He shouts 'Don't you know the dinosaur – the
    dinosaur is dead?'
Well, I know when grown-ups tell you things, they
    like you to agree
But still my Heterodontosaurus
My Heterodontosaurus
My Heterodontosaurus is the dinosaur for me.

37

They never will believe me and my brother thinks I'm
  mad,
My mum says I'll grow out of it and as for my old dad,
He yells at me 'You must have cotton wool between
  your ears
Because no one's seen a dinosaur for seventy million
  years!'
But I have got a dinosaur that no one else can see
It's my Heterodontosaurus
My Heterodontosaurus
My Heterodontosaurus is the dinosaur for me.

My dinosaur's a dancer, she's nimble and she's neat
As she dances down to meet me on her dainty, birdy
  feet,
As she dances round to greet me with her cheeky,
  beaky grin
And she gurgles when I tickle where she hasn't got a
  chin.
Yes, of all those curious creatures that ever used to be
The Heterodontosaurus
The Heterodontosaurus
The Heterodontosaurus is the dinosaur for me.

The Dinosaurs Are Not All Dead
Charles Malam

The dinosaurs are not all dead.
I saw one raise its iron head
To watch me walking down the road
Beyond our house today.
Its jaws were dripping with a load
Of earth and grass that it had cropped.
It must have heard me where I stopped,
Snorted white steam my way,
And stretched its long neck out to see,
And chewed, and grinned quite aimiably.

I Saw . . .
Adrian Henri

I'm *sure*
I saw a Dinosaur
just across the road,
peeping out above Tesco
and the D.I.Y. Store.
I did,
just before:
there's an enormous foot-mark
on the car park
and a Ford Escort
squashed flat; apart from that
there's an awful mess
where it looks like something's tripped
over a skip.

There was
that awful sound, too,
just like thunder, or the noise
the bin-lorries make
when they chew up the rubbish.

Perhaps I should go and investigate.

On second thoughts,
I think I'll just wait.

Sabretooth

Tom Stanier

Sabretooth, oh Sabretooth,
You really are spectacular.
Sabretooth, oh Sabretooth,
You're very like Count Dracula.

The Dinosaur
Edward Lucie-Smith

This poem is too small, I fear,
   To hold a dinosaur.
I led him here, but he was there,
   And there was always more.

How can I hope to fit the beast
   Within this cage of metre?
He's fifty fathoms long, at least –
   A hamster would be neater.

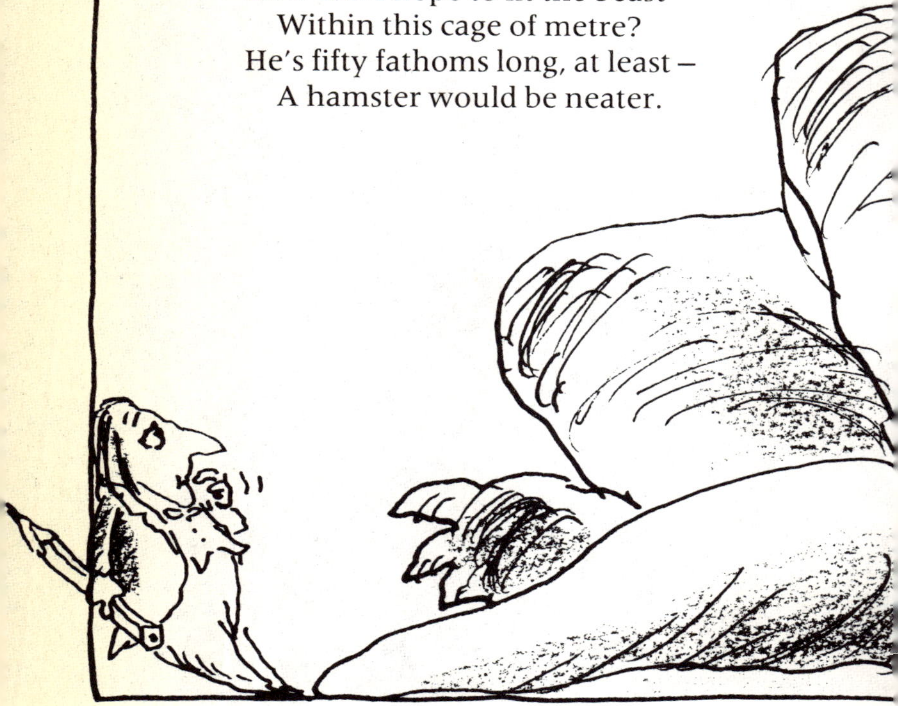

'Under the silver stars at night'
Catherine Baker

Under the silver stars at night
And under the deep dark sea
A creature might be lurking
Where no creature should be.

Somewhere beyond the reach of time
Where only the slow worms creep,
A creature may be stirring
Who has lain too long asleep.

He waited out the Ice Age,
He waited out the thaw,
He waited out the time of man
Alone on the ocean floor.

He knows his time is coming,
As sure as the old Earth turns;
As man is crumbling into dust
The dinosaur returns.

How the Dinosaur Got Here
Spike Milligan

'Daddy, what's a dinosaur?'
Said my daughter Jane.
'The dinosaur was a giant beast
That will never be seen again.'

'Where did they all come from?'
'Now that I cannot say.'
And at this information
She turned and walked away.

She must have thought about it,
For later that afternoon
She said to me, 'I know! I know!
They all came from the moon!'

'If that is true, my daughter,
Would you, pray, please tell
Exactly how they got here.'
She said, 'Of course – they fell!'

The Ichthyosaurus
Isabel Frances Bellows

There once was an ichthyosaurus
Who lived when the world was all porous,
But he fainted with shame
When he first heard his name,
And departed a long time before us.

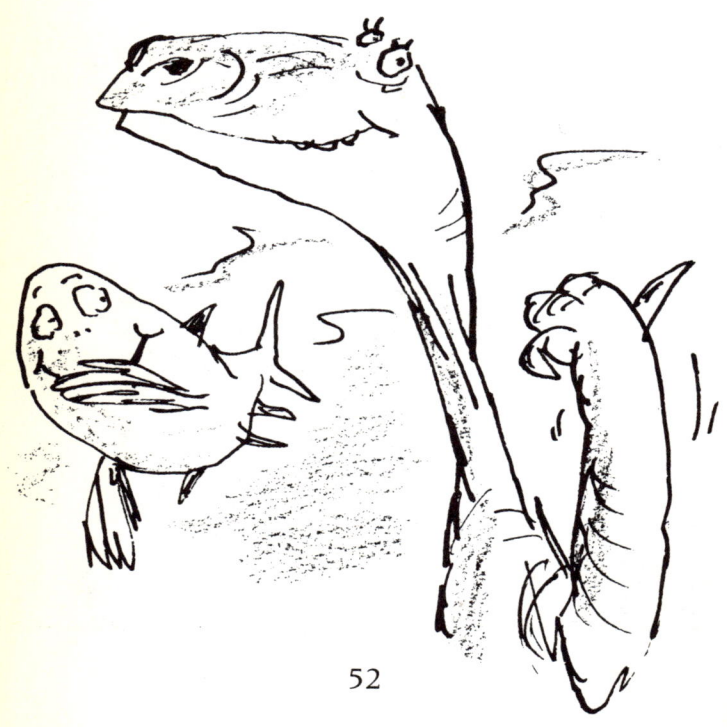

Dead and Alive
Leonard Clark

And in my dreams I sometimes see
a brontosaurus tracking me
with lashing tail and tiny head,
but I'm alive and he is dead.

He swam to many funerals
of other scaly animals,
but now he's turned to ribs of stone
and only left behind one bone.

Aliens in Time
Sam McBratney

When you look up on a clear night,
Do you think of time and stars?
Do you wonder if something
Rather strange
Is alive and well on Mars?

Near one of those twinkling suns up there,
Or beyond, in the deep of space,
Is an unknown creature opening
An eye
In what is – perhaps – a face?

And is there an island in the Universe
Where astronauts shall land,
And where the print of a giant foot
Lies waiting
In the interstellar sand?

But wherever starships go —
What could they find
To boggle the mind more,
Than Earth's own vanished Alien,
The Dinosaur?

Ode to an Extinct Dinosaur
Doug MacLeod

Iguanadon, I loved you,
With all your spiky scales,
Your massive jaws,
Impressive claws
And teeth like horseshoe nails.

Iguanadon, I loved you.
It moved me close to tears
When first I read
That you've been dead
For ninety million years.

Dinosaur Dip
Irene Rawnsley

Dinosaur
At the door
Ask him what he's knocking for
Little prickle in his paw
Made it tickle
Made it sore

Can't think of any more
Out Goes You!

Acknowledgements

'So Big' from *Songs for my Dog and Other People* by Max Fatchen (Kestrel Books, 1980), copyright © Max Fatchen, 1980. 'In China' by Mark Burgess, copyright © Mark Burgess, 1991. 'Tell all you know about . . .' by Margaret Ryan, copyright © Margaret Ryan, 1991. 'I'd Never Dine on Dinosaurs' from *The New Kid on the Block* by Jack Prelutsky (William Heinemann Ltd), copyright © Jack Prelutsky, 1984. 'Tricky Archaeopteryx' by Andrew Matthews, copyright © Andrew Matthews, 1991. 'Lament' by Derek Sampson, copyright © Derek Sampson, 1991. 'A Big Brontosaurus' from *Rhyme Time 2* by Barbara Ireson (Hutchinson), copyright © Barbara Ireson. 'Lizard' from *Come in to my Tropical Garden* by Grace Nichols (A & C Black), copyright © Grace Nichols. 'Pterodactyl' from *An Imaginary Menagerie* by Roger McGough, reprinted by permission of the Peters Fraser & Dunlop Group Ltd, copyright © Roger McGough. 'Destiny Dinosaur' by W. J. Corbett, copyright © W. J. Corbett, 1991. 'Where the Dinosaur Still Roams' by Hiawyn Oram, copyright © Hiawyn Oram, 1991. 'My Heterodontosaurus' by Leon Rosselson, copyright © Leon Rosselson, 1991. 'I Saw . . .' by Adrian Henri, copyright © Adrian Henri, 1991. 'Under the silver stars at night' by Catherine Baker, copyright © Catherine Baker, 1991. 'How the Dinosaur Got Here' from *Unspun Socks from a Chicken's Laundry* by Spike Milligan (Michael Joseph Ltd), copyright © Spike Milligan, 1981. 'Dead and Alive' by Leonard Clark, reprinted by permission of the Literary Executor of Leonard Clark. 'Aliens in Time' by Sam McBratney, copyright © Sam McBratney, 1991. 'Dinosaur Dip' by Irene Rawnsley, copyright © Irene Rawnsley, 1991. 'Ode to an Extinct Dinosaur' from *In the Garden of Bad Things* by Doug MacLeod. (Penguin Books Australia Ltd), copyright © Doug MacLeod.

Every effort has been made to trace all the copyright holders and the publishers apologise if any inadvertent omission has been made.